The Surrender at Appomattox

CORNERSTONES OF FREEDOM™

SECOND SERIES

Tom McGowen

Children's Press®
A Division of Scholastic Inc.
New York • Toronto • London • Auckland • Sydney
Mexico City • New Delhi • Hong Kong
Danbury, Connecticut

Photographs ©2004: Art Resource, NY/Private Collection, U.S.A: 40, 45 bottom; Bridgeman Art Library International Ltd., London/New York: 38 (Delaware Art Museum, Wilmington, USA), 7 (New York Historical Society, New York, USA), 30 (Private Collection); Corbis Images: 34 (Bettmann), 41 (Medford Historical Society Collection), 8 bottom, 8 top, 13, 18, 32, 33, 44 bottom; Hulton|Archive/Getty Images: 9, 24, 25, 37, 39; Library of Congress: 10 right, 14, 44 top right (via SODA), 4, 11, 21, 27; North Wind Picture Archives: 3, 5, 6, 10 left, 19, 22, 44 top left, 45 top right, 45 top left; Photri Inc.: cover bottom; PictureHistory.com: cover top, 17 right; Stock Montage, Inc.: 16 bottom, 28, 31; Courtesy of The Library of Virginia: 15, 16 top, 17 left; Town of Cape Elizabeth, Maine: 20; Virginia Historical Society, Richmond, Virginia: 36 (Copyright 1996, Lora Robins Collection of Virginia Art), 12.

Library of Congress Cataloging-in-Publication Data

McGowen, Tom.

The Surrender at Appomattox / Tom McGowen.

p. cm. — (Cornerstones of freedom. Second series)

Summary: Details the events that led to General Lee's surrender to General Grant at Appomattox Court House, bringing an end to the Civil War.

Includes bibliographical references (p.) and index.

ISBN 0-516-24231-8

1. Appomattox Campaign, 1865—Juvenile literature. 2. Lee, Robert E. (Robert Edward), 1807–1870—Juvenile literature. 3. Grant, Ulysses S. (Ulysses Simpson), 1822–1885—Juvenile literature. 4. United States—History—Civil War, 1861–1865—Peace—Juvenile literature. [1. Appomattox Campaign, 1865. 2. Lee, Robert E. (Robert Edward), 1807–1870. 3. Grant, Ulysses S. (Ulysses Simpson), 1822–1885. 4. United States—History—Civil War, 1861-1865.] I. Title. II. Series.

E477.67.M38 2003

973.7'38—dc21

2003009093

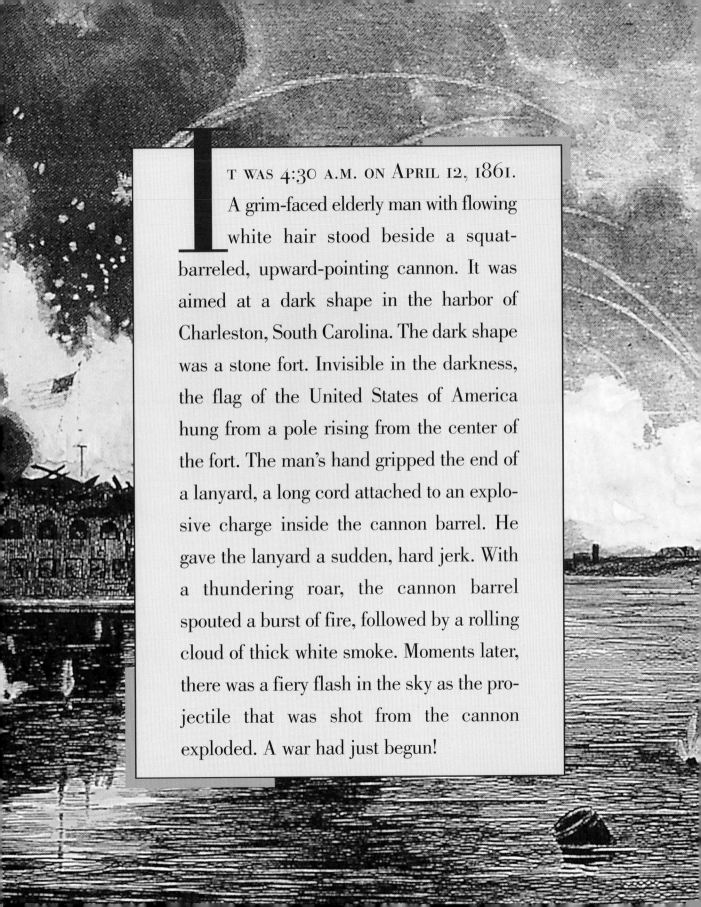

IT WAS 4:30 A.M. ON APRIL 12, 1861. A grim-faced elderly man with flowing white hair stood beside a squat-barreled, upward-pointing cannon. It was aimed at a dark shape in the harbor of Charleston, South Carolina. The dark shape was a stone fort. Invisible in the darkness, the flag of the United States of America hung from a pole rising from the center of the fort. The man's hand gripped the end of a lanyard, a long cord attached to an explosive charge inside the cannon barrel. He gave the lanyard a sudden, hard jerk. With a thundering roar, the cannon barrel spouted a burst of fire, followed by a rolling cloud of thick white smoke. Moments later, there was a fiery flash in the sky as the projectile that was shot from the cannon exploded. A war had just begun!

The "cotton culture" of the South continually demanded more land and more slaves, widening the gap between North and South.

A NATION DIVIDED

On that April morning, when American soldiers in gray uniforms opened fire on a fort defended by U.S. soldiers in blue uniforms, the Civil War began. It was to grind on for four long years. Historians offer different reasons as to why the Civil War began, but the rift between North and South likely came about as a result of great differences between their ways of life. The wealth of the North was based on industry, because many factories there turned out goods that could be sold throughout the world. The wealth of the

South depended on farming, and most farming was done by slaves. One of the major problems between the North and South concerned the ownership of slaves.

Before Abraham Lincoln (below) even reached the nation's capital to begin serving as president, the Confederacy had already been created and its leader, Jefferson Davis, elected. Lincoln's first task as president would be to direct the war against the Confederate states.

The fifteen Southern states allowed slavery, but the nineteen Northern states did not. Southerners felt outnumbered. They wanted slavery to be allowed in the new states that were being added to the United States in those days. But most people living in the Northern states and the Northern politicians who controlled the government wanted to make slavery illegal in the new states. Many Southerners felt this was a threat to their way of life and to their very freedom. They warned that if slavery were outlawed in the new states, the Southern states might simply secede, or withdraw from the United States, and form a separate nation that was free to make its own rules.

In 1860, presidential candidate Abraham Lincoln made it well known that he did not believe slavery should be allowed to spread into the new states. When Lincoln was elected on November 6, 1860, most Southerners believed the United States government had become their enemy. Southern states began to secede. During December 1860 and January 1861, six Southern states banded together and formed a new nation called the Confederate States of America, or the Confederacy. In March and April, five more Southern

BUILT FROM THE RUINS.

This banner was from the Secession Convention in Charleston, South Carolina, in 1861. South Carolina was the first state to secede in December 1860.

states joined the Confederacy. Jefferson Davis was elected president of the Confederacy, and an army was created to defend it.

Nineteen Northern states and four border states (states on the border between North and South) remained loyal to the United States government. Those states, together with the U.S. government, were known as the Union. The Union army was formed to force the South to end its **rebellion** and rejoin the Union. Lincoln feared that if the United States broke apart, it would show the world that a nation built on democracy could not last. He wanted to fight to keep the Union together, and so the Civil War began.

FOUR YEARS OF WAR

By the spring of 1865, the Confederacy was clearly losing the war. The South simply could not match the North's

The Civil War raged for four years and included some of the fiercest military campaigns in modern history.

This photograph, taken in 1864, shows a pair of captured Confederates, whose clothing hangs in tatters on their thin forms.

In contrast to the Confederates, Union soldiers were well dressed and well fed. This photograph was also taken in 1864.

★ ★ ★ ★

ability to produce weapons, equipment, and food. There were only two major Southern fighting forces left. One was a small army of about 27,000 men in North Carolina. The other was the main army of about 60,000 men in Virginia.

The Confederate soldiers were worn out. What was left of the men's uniforms was patched and ragged. Many men simply wore ordinary clothing of all kinds and did not even look like soldiers, except for their weapons and equipment. Making matters worse, food was scarce. Much of the fighting had taken place in Virginia, and many farms had been abandoned.

In contrast, the Union forces in Virginia, about 90,000 men, were well equipped, well dressed, and well fed. Supplies of food were brought to them daily from the North by ships. Their uniform was a coat of dark blue wool with

This photograph shows the Union Army of the Potomac's base in Yorktown, Virginia.

brass buttons and sky-blue wool trousers. They wore a blue cap with a visor and a round, flat top, officially known as a **forage** cap.

The Union forces in Virginia were split into two armies, known as the Army of the Potomac and the Army of the James, after two Virginia rivers. Each army had its own general, but both armies were under the overall command of General Ulysses S. Grant. Grant had served as an army officer from 1843 to 1854. When the Civil War began, he re-entered the army and was made a general. In 1864, he became General-in-Chief of all Union forces.

Many Northerners would come to view General Ulysses S. Grant (above left) as a hero because of his victories in several key battles. General Robert E. Lee's (above right) strong leadership and courage led him to become one of the most respected soldiers in our country's history.

The Confederate army in Virginia was called the Army of Northern Virginia. It was commanded by General Robert E. Lee, a Virginian, the supreme commander of all

Confederate forces. Lee had been in the U.S. Army since 1829, and when the war broke out, he was a lieutenant colonel. President Lincoln had originally offered Lee the job of commander of the Union army but, because he was from Virginia (now part of the Confederacy), Lee decided he could not fight against his own state and his own people. Instead, he became an officer of the Confederate army, and eventually became commander of the Army of Northern Virginia.

The cavalry, or horse soldiers, became one of the most important parts of the military during the Civil War. They could cover ground rapidly and also served as the "eyes" of the army, keeping abreast of the enemy's movements.

★ ★ ★ ★

REGIMENTS, MUSKETS, AND MINIÉ BALLS

A Civil War army was made up of infantry (foot soldiers), cavalry (horse soldiers), and artillery (cannons). The basic unit of an army was called a **regiment**. An infantry regiment was supposed to be formed of one thousand men, but by 1865, most regiments in both the North and South were down to a few hundred men. Four or five regiments were grouped together to form a **brigade**. Three or four brigades were put together to form a **division**. Two or three divisions formed a **corps**, and several corps made up an army.

Compared to the weapons of today, Civil War weapons were primitive. The main weapon used by soldiers on both sides was called a rifled musket. The word *rifled* means that inside the barrel—the long tube the bullet comes out of—there was a spiralled groove. This made the bullet spin, which made it travel

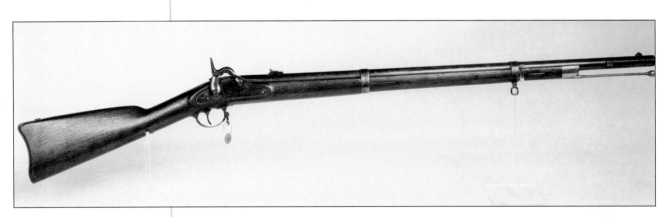

A musket had to be reloaded after each shot, which took a long time. Most soldiers could fire their musket only once or twice a minute.

straight instead of wobbling. A rifled musket could fire a lead bullet a distance of 750 yards (686 meters); however, in battle, men seldom fired at targets more than 200 yards (183 m) away.

The bullet, known as a minié ball after the French army officer who invented it, came wrapped in a paper tube called a cartridge. The cartridge was filled with sixty grains of black gunpowder. Each soldier carried a leather cartridge-box that held forty cartridges slung from his left shoulder by a strap. Fastened to his belt was a small leather pouch containing **percussion caps**. These were tiny cups of thin metal filled with an explosive charge. Pulling the trigger of a musket released

A Civil War soldier poses fully armed, holding a rifled musket and a leather pouch.

LOADING A MUSKET

To load a musket, a soldier tore open a cartridge and poured the powder into the musket barrel. With a long rod called a ramrod, he pushed the bullet down onto the powder. To cock the musket, the soldier pulled the hammer back so that it locked in position; he then fitted a percussion cap into place. He was now ready to fire, by pulling the trigger.

13

Cannons were particularly effective in hilly areas, where soldiers marched across low-lying, open fields nearby.

the gun's hammer, which then struck the percussion cap, causing a small explosion that detonated the gunpowder in the musket's barrel and shot the bullet out of the barrel.

Another important Civil War weapon was the cannon, a large gun mounted on a wooden, two-wheeled carriage. Civil War cannons fired solid iron balls that weighed from 6 to 24 pounds (2.7 to 10.8 kilograms), to a distance of 1,000 yards (914 m) or more. They also fired hollow metal projectiles called shells that were filled with gunpowder. The shells exploded in the air, sending metal fragments hurtling in all directions. Cannons were loaded and fired much like a musket.

A DESPERATE SITUATION

By April 1865, the Union army in Virginia had grown to 122,000 men; the Confederate Army of Northern Virginia only had some 60,000 men. On April 4, the Confederate army was clustered around a tiny town called Amelia Court House, named after the county courthouse building that stood in the town's center. Union forces were closing in on the town from the east and south.

General Lee knew he could never defeat the Union forces. His only hope was to travel south into North Carolina. His army could join with the southern army there, commanded by General Joseph Johnston. This might produce a force

The Union forces greatly outnumbered Lee's army.

The cavalry leading the Union army kept up attacks on Confederate troops.

Lee directed his troops southwest, toward North Carolina.

large enough to cause trouble for the Union army. At about noon on April 5, Lee started his troops marching southwest.

The Union commander, General Grant, guessed exactly what Lee had in mind. Grant started his forces marching as well. They moved alongside the southern army, but several miles away so the Confederates couldn't go directly south without running into Union forces. At the front of the Union army was General Philip Sheridan's cavalry corps, made up of 12,000 men. They kept up steady, hard-hitting attacks on the front of Lee's army, always forcing it to head west.

One of Lee's biggest problems was getting enough food for his soldiers. His army needed a supply of food every few days,

"LITTLE PHIL"

Union Major General Philip Sheridan (below) was only 5 feet 4 inches tall. He was known throughout the Union army as "Little Phil." However, he was tremendously respected and admired as a courageous and skillful cavalry leader.

so he had to arrange for food to be collected at places near where the army marched. His men were headed toward a town called Farmville, where a railroad passed through. The track ran to the city of Lynchburg, from which trains might bring food. Lee sent word to Lynchburg, asking for food to be sent to Farmville.

When the Southern troops reached Farmville on April 6, they were overjoyed to find food waiting for them. But their luck didn't last long. Part of Lee's army became separated, and Sheridan's cavalry plus two Union infantry corps struck with a vicious attack. Some six thousand Confederate soldiers were captured, and nearly two thousand more were killed or wounded. Lee was down to fewer than thirty thousand men. That night, he started his troops marching again.

The Union army was right on their heels. By the afternoon of April 7, Union infantry had entered Farmville, and General Grant set up his headquarters in a small hotel. Later, as Grant talked with one of his generals, he began to realize how bad things had become for General Lee. Abruptly, he announced that he would urge Lee to surrender,

This photograph shows a group of Confederate prisoners.

General Grant, shown here writing orders during a battle, took the first step toward ending the war.

or to give up and stop fighting. He called for paper, pen, and ink, and wrote out a historic message.

A CALL FOR SURRENDER

"General R. E. Lee, Commanding C.S. Army.
General: The results of the last week must convince
you of the hopelessness of further resistance on the
part of the Army of Northern Virginia in this struggle.

*I feel that it is so, and regard it as my duty to shift from myself the responsibility of any farther **effusion** of blood by asking of you the surrender of that portion of the Confederate States army known as the Army of Northern Virginia.*

U.S. Grant, Lieutenant General, Commanding Armies of the United States."

Brigadier General Seth Williams carried Grant's first message to Lee, asking him to surrender.

The message was given to an officer on Grant's **staff**, Brigadier General Seth Williams, to carry to Confederate lines. Williams took a soldier with him, who carried a white flag. This was known as a flag of truce, a symbol indicating that one army wanted to hold a peaceful meeting with the other. Soldiers were taught not to shoot at men carrying a white flag.

It was dark by the time Williams reached the edge of Confederate territory, and Southern soldiers keeping watch were nervous and suspicious. Suspecting a trick, they opened fire, and the soldier carrying the white flag was shot. Williams hid among some trees and called to the Southerners, explaining his mission. After a time, a young captain of a Georgia regiment called the Union messenger to come talk with him. Williams stepped out from hiding. He handed the captain Grant's message and asked that it be delivered quickly to Lee.

Lee was at his headquarters, a small house in the tiny town of Cumberland, with his second-in-command, General James Longstreet. Grant's message got to Lee at about ten o'clock. He read it and showed it to Longstreet, who studied it and said, "Not yet." Lee agreed.

Although he wasn't ready to surrender, Lee wanted to find out more about the terms Grant was willing to offer. The surrender of an army is a tremendously important event, one that can often bring an entire war to an end. Therefore, both sides must consider it very carefully. The side being asked to surrender generally wants to know what the terms of the surrender will be. Terms are what the army

LEE'S WARHORSE

General James Longstreet (left), Lee's second-in-command, was known to his troops as "Old Pete." General Lee referred to Longstreet as his warhorse, the name for a horse that had been through many battles.

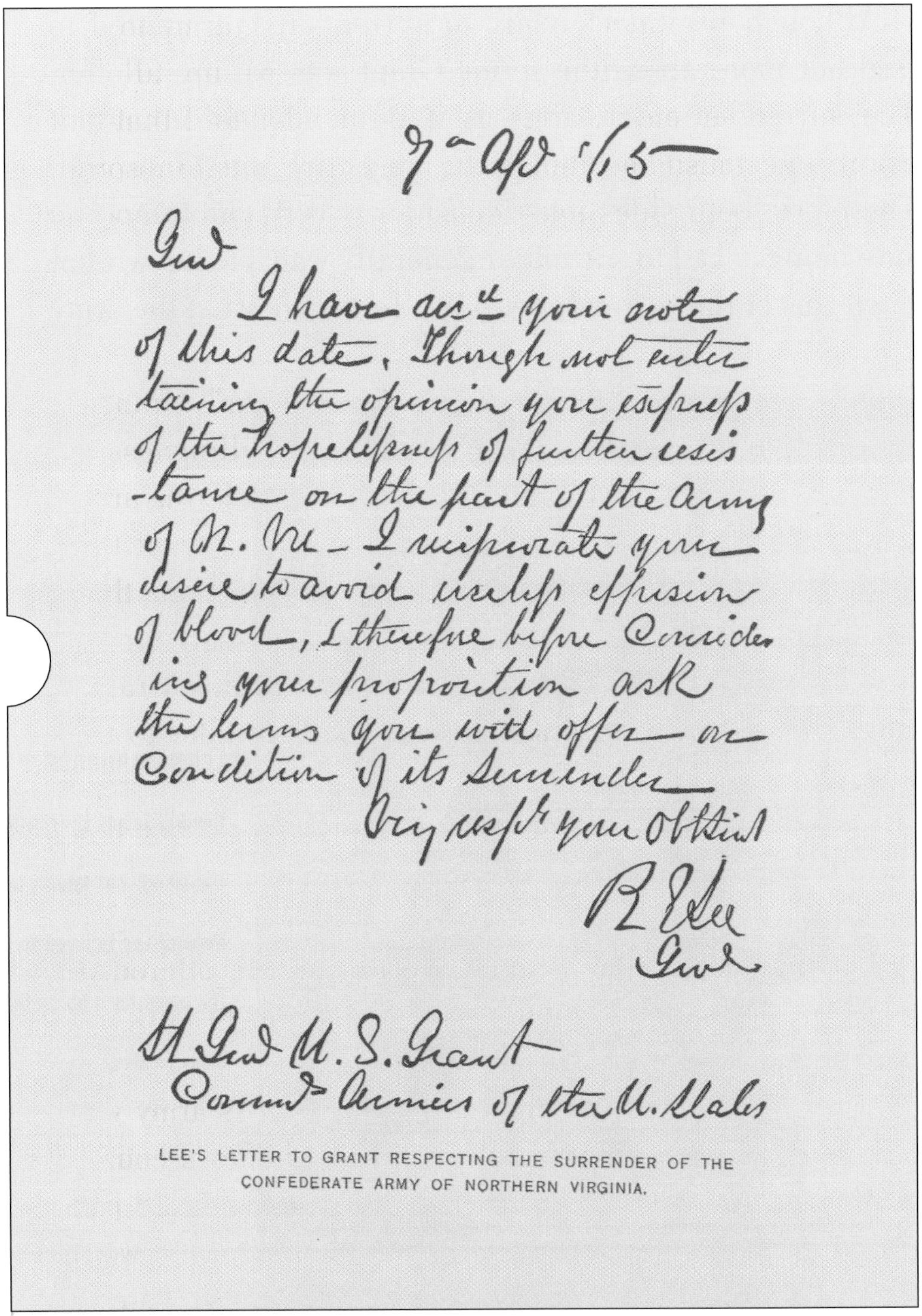

7ᵗʰ Apl '65 —

Genl

I have recd your note
of this date. Though not enter
taining the opinion you express
of the hopelessness of further resis
-tance on the part of the Army
of N. Va — I reciprocate your
desire to avoid useless effusion
of blood, I therefore before Consider
ing your proposition ask
the terms you will offer on
Condition of its Surrender —
                    Very respy your Obt Svt
                              R E Lee
                              Genl

Lt Genl U. S. Grant
Commd Armies of the U. States

LEE'S LETTER TO GRANT RESPECTING THE SURRENDER OF THE
CONFEDERATE ARMY OF NORTHERN VIRGINIA.

Shown here is Lee's letter to Grant inquiring about Grant's terms of surrender.

asking for a surrender wants the surrendering army to do. Usually, the surrendering army must give up all its weapons. Sometimes, a surrendering army is told that all its soldiers must become prisoners for a time. In some cases, a surrendering army is allowed to keep its weapons and simply march away in peace.

LEE ASKS A QUESTION

Grant's nickname—"Unconditional Surrender" Grant—implied that he was well known for his unwillingness to give any terms and would insist that the surrendering army do whatever he demanded. Lee wanted to find out if this was indeed true. He wrote a message to Grant saying that, although he did not agree it had become necessary for his army to surrender, he was interested in learning Grant's terms. He gave the message to an officer to take to the Union lines.

The next morning, Grant wrote a reply. He told Lee that the only terms he required would be that the men of the Army of Northern Virginia agree not to do any more fighting against the United States government. He offered to meet Lee, or anyone Lee might send, in order to work out a surrender.

Even as Grant was writing this message, Lee's army was marching toward another small town named after a county courthouse, Appomattox Court House. Lee was headed just beyond town to Appomattox Station. He had received word that four trains loaded with food had arrived there. Late in the afternoon, the Southern troops reached a point just

Appomattox Court House was a small town in rural central Virginia.

northeast of Appomattox Court House, where they halted to make camp. About this time, a messenger found Lee and gave him the letter from Grant.

LEE PLANS AN ATTACK

The terms Grant offered were much better than Lee had hoped. However, Lee was still not ready to surrender. Instead, he offered to meet Grant somewhere to discuss ways of making peace.

The Union army's sudden attack surprised Lee's army, cutting them off from needed supplies.

As an officer rode off with Lee's reply, there was a sudden explosion of cannonfire to the southwest. It continued for a time, then abruptly stopped. At about nine o'clock, an officer rode into camp with the news: A Union cavalry division had made a sudden, smashing attack against the westernmost part of Lee's army. Hundreds of Confederate soldiers had been captured or driven off, and twenty-four cannons captured. Union troops were now in control of the countryside between Lee's army and Appomattox Station, leaving no way for Lee to reach the supplies he had been counting on. Worse yet, his army was in danger of being surrounded.

Lee called his generals together. They decided there were only two choices. They could either surrender or make one last, desperate attempt to break through Sheridan's cavalry and head southwest. They decided to try the breakout. Lee immediately began sending out orders. His plan was to send a force of infantry and cavalry, commanded by Major General John Gordon, to push Sheridan's cavalry out of the way. Then the Confederate army would be able to move up the road and escape.

Meanwhile, Grant received Lee's message at midnight. He was wide awake, suffering from a splitting headache. He read what Lee had to say and shook his head in disappointment. Grant had no authority to discuss peace between the North and South, as Lee wanted to do. Only the president or members of the government could do that. "I will reply in the morning," he told his officers, then settled back to try to go to sleep.

ONLY ONE CHOICE

In the morning, with pain still pounding in his head, Grant wrote out a third message to Lee. He explained that while he had no authority to discuss peace terms, as Lee had suggested, he believed that Lee's surrender would lead to peace.

Lee continued to direct his army to battle, hoping to avoid surrender.

Grant continued to communicate with Lee, Knowing that Lee's situation worsened with each passing day.

However, the Confederate army was now on the move, beginning its attack. Three Southern infantry divisions, about five thousand men, with cavalry moving alongside on the right, trotted up the road. They saw nothing in their path but a brigade of Union cavalry— fewer than one thousand men. The cavalrymen starting falling back, and the Southerners began to howl in triumph.

Suddenly, the confident yells stopped short. An enormous force of blue-clad soldiers appeared over the hills beyond the road, regiment after regiment of Union infantry. They spread out on the hillsides with scores of cannons massed among them. The Union Army of the James had arrived, and the Confederate army's chance to break through was gone. The Southern attack came to a halt. To go on would have meant certain death for hundreds of men.

Lee knew that all hope was gone. He had only one choice—to surrender, which meant that the Confederacy had lost the war. "There is nothing left for me to do but go and see General Grant," he told his generals, "and I would rather die a thousand deaths!"

STEPS TOWARD SURRENDER

At 8:30 A.M., Lee mounted his horse and rode toward the Union lines with his secretary, Lieutenant Colonel Charles Marshall, Lieutenant Colonel Walter Taylor, Sergeant George Tucker, and some private soldiers. The sergeant

A CIVIL WAR ATTACK

To attack, each regiment of a brigade would form two lines. The regiments would move forward, one after another, about 75 yards (68.5 m) apart. The men moved at a running pace, shouting or howling to make as much noise as possible.

Custer receiving the flag of Truce — 1865

This pencil sketch shows a Confederate approaching Union lines under a flag of truce.

carried a stick with a dirty white handkerchief tied to it as a flag of truce. Before long, Lee and the others saw two Union soldiers on horseback coming toward them, one also carrying a flag of truce.

The Union soldiers were bringing the third message from General Grant to General Lee. Lee read it, then composed a message to Grant requesting a meeting to discuss surrender, and sent it off. The first step toward the surrender of the Army of Northern Virginia had been taken.

Within about an hour, more Union soldiers approached with a flag of truce. The man in command of this truce party was Lieutenant Colonel Orville Babcock, one of General Grant's **aides**. Grant had received Lee's message and responded, saying he was willing to meet with Lee wherever Lee wanted.

The nearest town was Appomattox Court House, so Lee sent Colonel Marshall and Private Joshua Johns there to look for a suitable meeting place. As they walked through

This drawing shows the meeting between Lee and Grant's aide, Lieutenant Colonel Babcock, which led to the surrender meeting in Appomattox Court House.

THE MAN WHO COULDN'T ESCAPE FROM WAR

In 1861, Wilmer McLean lived near Manassas Junction, Virginia, where the first major battle of the Civil War was fought. In 1863, he moved to Appomattox Court House, and in 1865, the last major event of the war occurred in his home.

This photograph of General Lee was taken some time after the surrender.

town, they met a man walking down the street, and Marshall asked if he knew of a house that could be used as a meeting place for the two generals. The man, Wilmer McLean, first took Marshall to an abandoned house, which the colonel felt was not good enough. McLean then took Marshall to his own home, a two-story red-brick building

For several days after the surrender on April 9th, the McLean house served as a meeting place and headquarters as the war came to an end.

with a wooden porch. He showed Marshall into the parlor, a special room for entertaining guests. Marshall decided it was perfect for the meeting and sent Johns to show General Lee the way.

General Lee soon arrived with Colonel Babcock and another Union officer. He sat down in an armchair near one of the windows. The Union officer went to wait outside for General Grant.

THE MEETING THAT MADE HISTORY

As Grant entered the parlor, Lee stepped forward to meet him. The two men shook hands. After a few moments of polite conversation, Lee said, "I suppose, General Grant, that the object of our present meeting is fully understood. I asked to see you to **ascertain** upon what terms you would receive the surrender of my army."

Lee and Grant wrote down the terms of surrender to make them official.

Grant answered that the terms were the same as he had put in his last message to Lee. Lee then suggested that Grant write them out, making them official, and that he would write out a statement accepting them. Grant agreed. One of Grant's officers picked up a small table and brought it to where the general was sitting. Grant placed his notebook on the table and began to write.

Grant's terms stated that all the officers and men of the Army of Northern Virginia were to agree that they would no longer bear weapons against the United States. All the Southern artillery, rifles, and army property were to be turned over to Union troops. Then, the Southerners were free to return home without fear of punishment.

As Lee read the terms, he became concerned. It seemed that all the military belongings of the Southern soldiers would have to be given up, including the horses. He explained that while most horses used in the U.S. Army were government property, most of the horses used by the Confederate army belonged to the men who rode them. Many of these men would go back to being farmers once they returned home. They would need their horses for planting and plowing crops.

Grant quickly assured Lee that he would order his officers to let the Southern men keep their horses. Lee appeared relieved. "This will have the best possible effect upon the men," he said warmly. "It will be very **gratifying**, and will do much toward **conciliating** our people."

THE SURRENDER THAT ENDED THE WAR

Grant turned to one of his officers and asked him to make a copy of the terms in ink. Lee had Colonel Marshall write his reply. It stated that Lee understood the terms, accepted them, and would have his army carry them out. Both Grant and Lee signed the documents, and the two papers were exchanged.

The surrender was complete by about 3:45 P.M. The two generals stood up and shook hands once again. Lee then bowed toward the other Union officers, turned away, and left the room. The warfare between the Union army and the Army of Northern Virginia was over.

Grant and Lee shook hands after the signing of the surrender terms.

The surrender of Lee's army ultimately signaled the end of the Civil War. This illustration shows Lee and Grant going their separate ways after the meeting.

As Lee stepped out onto the porch, several Union officers came to attention and saluted. This is known as military courtesy—the saluting of a higher-ranking officer, even one from an enemy army. Lee saluted in return and walked down the steps. He mounted his horse and began riding away. When Lee reached the Southern army's position, soldiers crowded around him.

This painting by A.R.H. Ranson shows General Lee retreating from Appomattox Court House with his army following, some weeping and sobbing in defeat.

* * * *

"Are we surrendered?" they asked anxiously.

Lee halted his horse. Tears were streaming from his eyes.

"Men, we have fought the war together and I have done the best I could for you," he said. Then he told them they were going home. Some men began to curse, others began to cry. Some begged Lee to let them continue fighting. But Lee rode on silently.

Things were very different in the Union lines. General Meade flung himself onto a horse and galloped down the road, waving his hat. "It's all over boys!" he yelled. "Lee's surrendered!"

The Union soldiers had awakened that morning fully expecting to fight a battle. Now, suddenly, they had been saved. Men began to shout with joy. They danced and flung themselves about, hugging one another. They were over-joyed to be alive. The war was over!

Joyous families greeted Union soldiers coming home after the war.

THE COST OF THE WAR

More than 600,000 men died during the Civil War—almost as many as in all of the United States' other wars combined. Not all the deaths were from battle. More than half were caused by disease, such as dysentery, typhoid, pneumonia, and infected wounds.

A CEREMONY OF SURRENDER

The surrender of an army at that time was an extremely important ceremony in which the soldiers gave up their weapons and equipment. On April 12, the Army of Northern Virginia marched up the road to Appomattox Court House, one regiment after the next. The road was lined with Union soldiers, and the two sides saluted one another.

The Confederate regiments halted, and the men began to stack their muskets. The men then hung their ammunition boxes from the tops of each stack. They were now without weapons and were no longer soldiers.

The men who had carried their regiment's flags carefully rolled the flags up and placed them on one of their regiment's rifle stacks, as property of the Union army. Some regiments, however, had burned the flags or buried them in secret places rather than turn their flags over to the enemy.

Confederate soldiers were required to hand over their flags after the surrender. While many flags were surrendered to the Union army, others were burned or hidden. The flag symbolized the bloodshed and glory of the many battles that were fought for their beliefs.

At the end of the Civil War, much of the South was left in ruins, with some cities and towns completely destroyed. It would take many years to rebuild and strengthen the region.

Lee's surrender essentially brought the war to an end. Not long after, General Johnston's army surrendered to Union forces in North Carolina, and other small Confederate forces surrendered in Alabama and Mississippi. The Confederacy no longer existed, and there was peace throughout the South.

The surrender at Appomattox brought peace, but the South had been ruined by the war. Cities had been damaged by fire and bombardment, railroad lines had been destroyed, and farms had been abandoned and overgrown. Many people were homeless and starving. For many years, there was great bitterness and hatred between the people of the South and North. Gradually, these feelings faded away.

The surrender at Appomattox was one of the most important events in United States history. It meant that slavery would soon be brought to an end. It also meant that the United States would remain a single nation with one central government. Thus, it helped put the United States on the path toward becoming the strong and important country that it is today.

A PRESIDENT DIES

Five days after the surrender at Appomattox Court House, President Abraham Lincoln was assassinated—shot and killed by a man named John Wilkes Booth. Booth, who had supported the Confederacy, believed that Lincoln had started the war.

Glossary

aides—officers who assist a general or other high-ranking officer in his work

ascertain—to make sure of something

brigade—an army organization formed of several infantry regiments and commanded by a colonel or brigadier general

conciliating—regaining trust and friendship

corps—an army organization formed of several divisions and commanded by a major general

division—an army organization formed of several brigades and commanded by a brigadier general

effusion—the pouring out of a liquid

forage—to search for food or provisions

gratifying—pleasing

percussion cap—an explosive device that detonates, or explodes, when struck

rebellion—organized opposition to a government or people in power

regiment—an army organization formed of either ten companies (infantry), or twelve (cavalry), commanded by a lieutenant-colonel or colonel

staff—a group of officers who assist with the administration of an organization

Timeline: The Surrender

1865

APRIL 4
Union forces close in on the Confederate Army of Northern Virginia near Amelia Court House.

APRIL 5
The Confederate army begins a march to Farmville. The Union army follows alongside.

APRIL 6
The Confederate army reaches Farmville, but a portion of the army is cut off by Union infantry and cavalry. The Confederates leave for Appomattox Station.

APRIL 7
The Union army enters Farmville. General Grant decides to ask General Lee to surrender. Lee receives Grant's message and sends a message back, asking about terms.

APRIL 8
Grant answers, presenting his terms. Lee refuses to surrender, but wants to talk about peace. Union cavalry cut Lee off from Appomattox Station. Lee decides to attempt a breakout.

at Appomattox

APRIL 9
Lee's breakout attempt fails; he decides he must surrender. Lee and Grant meet in Appomattox Court House. The surrender is signed, signaling the end of the war.

APRIL 12
The Army of Northern Virginia officially surrenders, turning in its weapons and equipment. The Confederate soldiers leave to go home.

APRIL 14
President Abraham Lincoln is assassinated.

APRIL 26
Confederate General Joseph Johnston surrenders all remaining troops under his command to Union General William T. Sherman. The Confederacy no longer exists. The United States is once again one nation.

To Find Out More

BOOKS

Beller, Susan Provost. *Billy Yank and Johnny Reb: Soldiering in the Civil War*. Brookfield, CT: Twenty-First Century Books, 2000.

Dolan, Edward. *The American Civil War: A House Divided*. Brookfield, CT: Millbrook Press, 1997.

Gaines, Ann Graham. *The Confederacy and the Civil War in American History*. Berkeley Heights, NJ: Enslow Publishers, 2000.

Hull, Mary E. *The Union and the Civil War in American History*. Berkeley Heights, NJ: Enslow Publishers, 2000.

Marrin, Albert. *Virginia's General: Robert E. Lee and the Civil War*. New York, Atheneum, 1994.

ONLINE SITES

Gettysburg National Military Park's Civil War Page for Kids
http://www.nps.gov/gett/gettkidz/kidzindex.htm

Appomattox Court House National Historical Park
http://www.nps.gov/apco/

American Experience, Ulysses S. Grant
http://www.pbs.org/wgbh/amex/grant/

Index

Bold numbers indicate illustrations.

About the Author

Tom McGowen is a children's book author with a special interest in military history, on which he has written seventeen previous books. His most recent book in the Cornerstones of Freedom Series was *The 1968 Democratic Convention*. As an author of more than sixty books for young readers, fiction and nonfiction, he has received the Children's Reading Round Table Annual Award for Outstanding Contributions to the Field of Children's Literature.